A *fashionable* HISTORY of DRESSES & SKIRTS

A FASHIONABLE HISTORY OF DRESSES & SKIRTS
was produced by

David West 𐀀 **Children's Books**

7 Princeton Court
55 Felsham Road
London SW15 1AZ

Author: Helen Reynolds
Editor: Clare Hibbert
Picture Research: Carlotta Cooper
Designer: Julie Joubinaux

First published in Great Britain in 2003 by
Heinemann Library, Halley Court, Jordan Hill,
Oxford OX2 8EJ, a division of
Harcourt Education Ltd.

OXFORD MELBOURNE AUCKLAND
JOHANNESBURG BLANTYRE GABORONE
IBADAN PORTSMOUTH (NH) USA CHICAGO

Copyright © 2003 David West Children's Books

07 06 05 04 03
10 9 8 7 6 5 4 3 2 1

ISBN 0 431 18333 3 (HB)
ISBN 0 431 18341 4 (PB)

British Library Cataloguing in Publication Data

Reynolds, Helen
A fashionable history of dresses and skirts
1. Dresses - History - Juvenile literature 2. Skirts
- History - Juvenile literature 3. Fashion - History
- Juvenile literature
I. Title II. Dresses and skirts
391'.009

Printed and bound in China

PHOTO CREDITS :
Abbreviations: t-top, m-middle, b-bottom, r-right,
l-left, c-centre.

Front cover m & 19br – Rex Features Ltd; tl,
3 & 12 bl – Dover Books; r & 14l – Mary
Evans Picture Library.
Pages 4tr, 7tr, 9br, 12mr, 21tr, 25br – The Culture
Archive. 4-5b, 6-7, 7m, 18br, 22tr & br, 26tr –
Dover Books. 5bm & 21l, 5br, 11tr, 13br, 15 all,
17 both, 19b, 21br, 22bl, 22-23, 23r, 26tl, 27br,
29tl – Rex Features Ltd. 6tr & bl, 8tr & br, 8-9,
9tr, 10tr, 12tl, 13tl, 16tr, 16-17, 18tl, 20tl,
20-21, 24bl, 24-25b, 25tr, 26bl, 27l, 28 both –
Mary Evans Picture Library. 7br – Digital Stock.
10bl, 11ml, 14mr, 16bl – Hulton Archive. 11bl –
Irving Solero/The Museum at the Fashion
Institute of Technology. 13bm – Karen Augusta,
www.antique-fashion.com. 19l – V&A Picture
Library. 24tl – © National Trust Photographic
Library/Derrick E. Witty. 28-29b – Corbis
Images. 29tr & br – Katz/FSP.

*An explanation of difficult words can be
found in the glossary on page 31.*

A *fashionable* HISTORY of DRESSES & SKIRTS

Heinemann
LIBRARY

Contents

MAKING A DEARSKIN DRESS

Native American Indians hunted animals for food. But they made full use of their kill, stitching soft, warm clothes from the skin.

GREEK TUNIC

Dress in ancient times involved little sewing. This 19th-century copy of a Greek tunic, or chiton, is pinned at the shoulders and belted at the waist.

From skins to PVC

THE ORIGINS OF DRESSES AND SKIRTS can be seen in the animal skins worn by early people. Later, with the first civilizations, people learned to make cloth, which they draped around the body. Cloth was a prized item. Great thought went into not wasting any. This became less important as cloth-making techniques improved. Tailors could show off their skills with ever more complicated – but often uncomfortable – styles.

Then, in the 20th century, women began to lead more active lifestyles. They demanded clothes that were easier to wear, and more practical. Plainer styles also came with advances in man-made fabrics. The latest materials do not need lots of clever cuts and seams to make dresses or skirts that hold their shape. They are ideal for simple, figure-hugging clothes.

DESIGNER EVENING-DRESS

A designer dress like this one, worn by Halle Berry (by the designer Mischka c.2001) is made from exquisite, expensive fabrics. It is cut to fit the body of the wearer exactly.

PVC MINI-DRESS

From shiny PVC to stretchy Lycra, man-made materials give us a wider choice of clothing than ever before.

Wrapping

THE FIRST DRESSES AND SKIRTS were simply lengths of cloth wrapped around the body. As people became more skilled – and more interested in how they looked – the cloth was draped and folded, pleated, tucked and knotted. Clothing showed off both the body and the fabric. The ancient Egyptians, Persians, Greeks and Romans all wrapped their clothes around their bodies.

Classical cloaks

Ancient civilizations turned wrapping into an art form. The Greek cloak, or himation, was a large rectangle of cloth wrapped around the body and pinned at the shoulder with a brooch. The Romans used an enormous half circle of material to make their toga. It was wound around the body so that it fell in complex folds.

ROMAN TOGAS
Roman men wore outer garments called togas on special occasions. Ordinary citizens wore white ones. Only the Roman emperor's toga was rich purple, coloured with expensive dyes.

Wrapping up warm

Long after the Roman empire fell, people still created clothes by wrapping – but styles were simpler. The Saxons, Danes and Celts wrapped extra layers of cloth around the body to keep out the cold. These cloaks, or mantles, were worn right up to the Middle Ages.

Design on the stand

The ancient art of wrapping is used in haute couture dressmaking. Material is wrapped round the tailor's dummy, or stand, then cut and pinned back together to recreate the garment's shape. Next, the design on the stand is dismantled so a paper pattern can be made. Before computer-generated design, this approach to dressmaking was the only way to create in three dimensions.

'Design on the stand' reached its peak in the 1930s – a time of flowing, draped dresses. A master of this method was the French couturier Alix Grès (1903–93), who had originally trained as a sculptor. Her imaginative, Greek-style evening-gowns were cleverly wrapped and draped to create beautiful, asymmetric (irregular) shapes.

A GRÈS CREATION

Grès favoured soft, fluid fabrics such as jersey and silk. These complemented her draping technique beautifully.

THE VERSATILE SARI

The traditional dress of Indian women is the sari, a five-metre length of cotton or silk that wraps around the body. The end flicks over the shoulder, or pulls over the head as a scarf.

SET IN STONE

Master stonemasons carved this statue of the Buddha long ago. But Buddhist monks today still wear simple, flowing robes.

WEARING SARONGS, ECUADOR

In hot countries, a simple, wraparound sarong is cool and comfortable.

The tunic

THE TUNIC IS ONE OF THE SIMPLEST FORMS OF DRESS. *The Greeks and Romans wore it, tied round the waist with a cord or girdle. Tunics have come down through the centuries and been adapted by different cultures and in different times. The tunic has proved to be one of the most versatile of all garments, whether in its simplest, draped form or refined by fashions.*

Clothing for all classes

In Britain, the tunic changed little from the time of Roman rule (CE 43–400) right up to the Norman Conquest (1066). It was worn by everyone – serfs, yeoman farmers and the nobility. It was even worn by soldiers as a surcoat (outer garment) over their chain mail. It remained the basic dress of both sexes until the 1300s. Then, people dropped the tunic for more complex garment styles.

THE BAYEUX TAPESTRY

The Bayeux Tapestry tells us about events that led up to the Norman Conquest – but that's not all. It also provides a record of the clothes people wore at the time.

KNIGHTS HOSPITALLERS

These medieval knights wore a tunic and cloak even when dressed for battle. The Hospitallers took part in the Crusades, but they also cared for the sick.

Monk's habit

The costume worn by a monk is called a habit. Franciscan friars wear plain brown tunics in coarse, hard-wearing fabric.

The haute couture tunic

At the beginning of the 20th century the basic tunic shape came back into fashion. French couturier Paul Poiret (1879–1944) drew inspiration from oriental-style tunics. His collections starred baggy harem pants worn under lampshade tunics, so-called because they were wired at the bottom to stand out in a circle around the body. Poiret's striking clothes were made in rich, exotic fabrics, such as silks, brocades and velvets.

Sixties style

The mini-skirted tunic became the height of fashion during the 1960s. It was teamed with skinny-rib sweaters or blouses. Made in the latest synthetic fabrics, such as Crimplene and nylon, tunic mini-dresses had a stiff, strong silhouette.

Russian peasant dress

Up until World War I, Russian women wore simple, belted tunics like these. The tunic remains an important part of traditional dress in many countries.

School tunics

During the 1920s and 1930s, schoolgirls wore box-pleated tunics over a blouse and tie. Tunics were made in sensible, dark gabardine – a hard-wearing wool and cotton mix that would not show the dirt.

The tailored dress

IN EUROPE IN THE MIDDLE AGES *the cut of women's dresses became more sophisticated. Tailors put in seams to give garments more shape. At first, fashionable dresses followed the natural contours of the body – later on, women would have to mould themselves to the dress shape!*

Fit for a princess

In the second half of the 19th century a dress style was introduced that was shaped without a waist seam. It fitted tightly around the bust, then the skirt had an extra piece of fabric, or gore, sewn in so that it flared out over the bustle. Cut in panels from shoulder to hem, this style was named the princess dress in honour of Alexandra, Princess of Wales (1844–1925). A variation was the princess polonaise, in which the skirt was drawn up at the back to reveal a frilly underskirt.

NOBLEWOMAN'S GOWN

High ranking ladies of the 1300s wore dresses with trains. Over the tunic is an unbelted over-gown which is tailored in at the waist. The long, streamer sleeves were called tippets.

Seamed shapes

Princess-style seaming became popular again in the 1950s. The trapeze line used panels to create a dress shaped like a trapezium. The neckline and hem were parallel while the sides tapered out, like the sides of a triangle. The A-line was very similar, tailored in the shape of a letter 'A'. Introduced in 1955 by Christian Dior (1905–57), this flattering shape has since been revisited by many designers.

PRINCESS ALEXANDRA & HER DAUGHTERS

Alexandra married Britain's future King Edward VII in 1863. She is pictured here with their daughters Louise, Victoria and Maud. As Princess of Wales, Alexandra gave her name to the princess dress. This style used diagonal seaming so that the dress fitted snugly at the top, then widened so a crinoline and bustle fitted under the skirt.

Vionnet outfit

This 1920s dress and matching cape demonstrate Madeleine Vionnet's clever, flowing lines. A snug-fitting cloche hat, beaded clutch bag and elegant, high heels complete the look.

Long & lean eveningwear

In the 1930s, women adored romantic, floor-sweeping evening gowns that showed off their curves. Sometimes they would add a short jacket with smart, padded shoulders.

Cut to fit

One 20th-century designer who made dresses that adapted to the wearer's body (rather than the other way round) was Madeleine Vionnet (1876–1975). She achieved her legendary fit with unusual seaming. As Vionnet clothes were bias-cut (cut across the grain of the cloth), they seemed limp and shapeless – until they were put on! Then they transformed into smooth, fluid dresses. Not as famous as her contemporaries Coco Chanel (1883–1971) and Elsa Schiaparelli (1890–1973), Vionnet is nevertheless regarded as the master of the dress and its construction.

A-line woollen mini-dress

This dress was designed by André Courrèges (b.1923) in the late sixties. Courrèges achieves the A-line silhouette with hardly any visible seams. The rounded pockets and belt buckle contrast with the overall angular shape.

The waist

FASHION IS A GRADUAL PROCESS OF CHANGE. One of the most prominent changes in the shape of European women's dress came during the Renaissance. Women's waists gained more prominence as the belted medieval dress was replaced by a fitted bodice, worn over a gathered skirt.

Waist watchers!

The Renaissance was a time of great prosperity. In England, the Tudor dynasty held the throne and trade flourished. Beautiful cloths were produced, including sumptuous velvets and elaborate silk brocades.

These fabrics were heavy, stiff and totally unsuitable for the flowing gowns that had been fashionable in medieval times. Instead, tailors used them to create more structured styles that emphasized the waist.

In the following centuries the waist position fluctuated but always remained defined. The waist reached its highest point around 1800 with the empire, or directoire, line. The look was inspired by classical Roman dress, following the exciting discoveries made at Pompeii from the mid-1700s.

ELIZABETHAN DRESS

Only a wealthy woman could have owned this dress of 1583. The bodice and skirt are in rich brocade; the ruff and cuffs are in costly lace.

WORTH GOWN

Crinolines and bustles were made popular by Charles Frederick Worth (1825–95). He dressed all the most fashionable ladies in Paris, including the Empress Eugénie (1826–1920).

DIRECTOIRE DRESS

The fine, gauzy dresses popular during the Directoire period had high waists that began just below the bust. This look was made popular by the Empress Joséphine (1763–1814), first wife of Napoleon Bonaparte (1769–1821).

_H_igh, low or somewhere in the middle...
Dress styles returned the waist to its proper place by around 1850. Waists were accentuated by immensely wide skirts, supported on a cage of crinoline. In the 1900s, waists rose in a classical revival, then in the 1920s they fell to hip level with flapper fashions.

Following World War II (1939–45), Christian Dior introduced his New Look in 1947. Romantic and glamorous, the style emphasized the waist with big, billowing skirts.

_A_ DRESS TO DANCE IN

Flappers were the fashionable young women of the 1920s, known for their shockingly short haircuts – and high hemlines! With its drop-waist and fringed hem, this dress gave a flapper perfect freedom to enjoy the latest energetic dances, such as the charleston.

_D_IOR'S NEW LOOK

In 1947, Christian Dior created the New Look which really drew attention to the waist. After the rationing of World War II, this look was an instant sensation – the skirts used extravagant quantities of fabric!

The working wardrobe

THE VAST CRINOLINES OF THE VICTORIAN ERA *restricted women's movement. Two campaigners for more practical dress were the Americans Amelia Bloomer (1818–94) and Elizabeth Cady Stanton (1815–1902). They promoted the bloomer outfit – a knee-length, loose dress worn over baggy trousers (bloomers). Unfortunately, most people viewed the style as a joke. It was left to the Rational Dress Society (founded in London in 1881) to call for sensible fashions for women.*

Woollen suit

By the late 19th century, more and more women were working in offices. The most practical outfit was a suit, such as this trim, tailored jacket and skirt.

Utility wear

During World War II, labour and fabrics were scarce. Britain's Utility clothing was designed to be practical and hard-wearing. Manufacturers followed strict rules to avoid waste.

Suits make sense

Women finally began to wear more practical clothes as they started going out to work. Increasingly, women found jobs as typists and office workers. They needed outfits that looked smart but were also easy to wear and care for. 'Separates' made perfect fashion sense. By the end of the 19th century, these women had adapted the man's jacket, wearing it with a matching skirt, over a fine, lawn blouse. This became their working wardrobe. Today, the suit remains the professional woman's key outfit, though its exact styling changes as the seasons bring new fashions.

CHANEL TWEED SUIT

Karl Lagerfeld (b.1938) became design director at Chanel in 1983. This is one of his versions of the classic, boxy suits that made Coco Chanel famous.

POWER SUIT

'Power dressing' was a term coined in the 1980s to describe the kinds of suits worn by successful businesswomen. This one by Yves Saint Laurent (b.1936) has the typical boxy shape, padded shoulders and short skirt.

PAUL SMITH SUIT

British designer Paul Smith (b.1946) gained a reputation for suiting up some of the world's movers and shakers early in the 21st century. Here the pencil skirt is still in evidence, although longer than the 1980s mini.

Straight & narrow

FROM THE 15TH CENTURY, *when the flowing medieval gown was dispensed with, until the 19th century most 'dresses' were in fact separates – bodices worn with a skirt and petticoat. During the 19th century, it became fashionable to wear a skirt in a heavier fabric with a lighter bodice or blouse. This was the beginning of the modern skirt.*

The search for a wearable skirt

In the early 20th century, designers looked at ways to make the skirt more comfortable. One mistaken design was Paul Poiret's hobble skirt of 1911. It was comfortably loose at the hips, but so tight at the ankle that walking was almost impossible! The hobble was shortlived, but caused an outcry.

After World War I, Jean Patou (1880–1936) and Coco Chanel began to make sporty clothes for active women. Stopping at the calf or knee, skirts often had pleats for easy movement.

THE LATEST SACK-RACE

Poking fun at the hobble

It was hard to move quickly in the hobble skirt because it was so tight around the calves. Wearers could only take very small steps – or jumps! Contemporary cartoonists had a field day.

Adapting the hobble

High society gathers for a cricket match in London, 1914. Just three years after its launch, the hobble skirt has already been reworked. The draped slit at the front frees the legs, so walking is easier.

Jersey suits in the styles of Chanel and Patou

Shorter, sportier skirts came into fashion in the 1920s. They were worn with loose, knitted cardigans or jackets.

Pencil skirt, 1950s

The knee-length straight skirt was very popular in the 1940s, because its shape used little fabric. In the 1950s the style lengthened and became known as the pencil skirt. It was usually teamed with a short, shaped jacket.

Sleek & chic

Throughout the 1920s the couturier Coco Chanel designed clothes that were comfortable, practical and sporty. Her loose cardigans and twinsets were teamed with straight, knee-length skirts. Although Chanel's designs were haute couture, their simple shape made them easy to copy. They quickly filtered down to the mass market.

Long, straight pencil skirts became particularly fashionable in the 1950s. Cheap to produce, they looked extremely elegant when worn with a jacket and high heels. Modelled by the most beautiful mannequins of the day, such as Fiona Campbell Walter (*b.*1932) and Barbara Goalen (1921–2002), pencil skirts were popular with women of all ages. They were a hit with the youth market when teamed with the latest, figure-hugging sweaters. This style was popularized in Hollywood by 'girl-next-door' actresses such as Lana Turner (1921–95).

Hobbled again!

In the 1990s, the long, slim hobble skirt returned. This time around clever cutting, slits or modern, stretchy Lycra made it far easier to walk in.

Popular pleats

PLEATS ARE FOLDS OF FABRIC *used as decoration, and also to provide fullness in dresses and skirts. They can do this in different ways. During the 18th century, loose-fitting sack dresses featured deep box pleats at the back, running from the neck to the hem. In contrast, the width of a 19th-century crinoline was achieved with rows and rows of neat pleats at the waistline.*

EVIDENCE OF EGYPTIAN PLEATS

Only a few scraps of linen dresses from ancient Egypt survive as evidence of pleating, but clothes in the many Egyptian wallpaintings and on contemporary statues are frequently intricately pleated.

Egyptian pleats

The ancient Egyptians are known for their beautiful, pleated clothes. Around 3,500 years ago, the cloaks, skirts and dresses worn by the Egyptian royalty and nobility were decorated with rows of fine pleats. Even commoners and slaves had simple pleats in the front of their skirts.

Victorian pleats

The Victorians loved decoration. Fine pin pleats decorated their lawn cotton blouses. And clothing designed to be worn for sports, such as bicycling, tennis or gymnastics, had roomy pleats to allow for ease of movement.

VICTORIAN SCHOOLGIRL DRESSED FOR THE GYM

In Britain, going to school became compulsory in the 1800s. New schools were built, all with gymnasiums. Physical education was an important part of the timetable at schools for both girls and boys.

Pleats are here to stay

Spanish-born designer Mariano Fortuny (1871–1949) patented his own special method of pleating in 1909. He used it to create his Delphos dress, a flowing gown made of tightly-pleated silk or velvet. The Delphos dress is a design classic that is still copied sometimes today.

Then, in the 1950s, chemists came up with ways to treat material so that pleats stayed in permanently. Swish skirts designed for dancing to the popular rock-'n'-roll music of the period featured accordion and sunray pleats.

*P*ERMANENT PLEATS

In this fine wool dress, designed in 1955, pressed pleats radiate out from the hip seam.

*F*ORTUNY'S *D*ELPHOS DRESS OF 1920

Fortuny's clever pleating made silk catch the light beautifully.

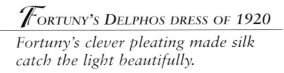

*R*OCKERS REUNION

Rock-'n'-roll fans get together in 1984, wearing accordion pleated skirts over full petticoats.

A glimpse of flesh

ONE OF THE REASONS WE WEAR CLOTHES *is to enhance our naked body. However, what looks beautiful to one generation or culture may appear ugly to the next. In different periods we have covered certain parts of our body while leaving others exposed. What we choose to expose depends on our culture – and current fashions, of course.*

Court dress

Low, square-cut bodices were fashionable in the 16th century. The stiff, tight-fitting fabric pushed up the breasts and showed off the cleavage.

A hint of cleavage

Excavations on Crete show that the Minoans may have worn elaborate, fitted dresses that exposed the breasts. Such a style is unusual – dresses from earliest times have modestly covered the breasts.

Low necklines that boldly reveal some cleavage have come in and out of fashion. In the 19th century the respectable woman was always well covered. However, couturier Charles Frederick Worth's extravagant designs included some daring eveningwear that had extremely low, or décolleté, necklines.

Camille Clifford, the Gibson Girl

Stage actress Camille Clifford (1885–1971) poses with her hair piled high to reveal a long neck, bare shoulders and a perfect hourglass figure. She was one of the Gibson Girls, drawn by artist Charles Gibson (1867–1944). His pen-and-ink drawings captured many fashionable women of the day.

Minis, midis & maxis

Unless you had thin legs, the miniskirt was a difficult fashion to wear. In the late 1960s, midis and maxis came along, giving women the option of exposing far less leg.

Sixties see-through

This mini-dress is made from semi-transparent plastic. The whole body is revealed if the light is right!

Backs, legs & tummies on show!

In the 20th century low necklines were not a key fashion feature, although 1930s evening-dresses had low backs. In the 1960s a complete transformation occurred when Mary Quant (*b.*1934) popularized the miniskirt, showing off more leg than ever before. Since then, designers have exposed just about every other body part, including the bare midriff. There have even been crazes for slashed, peephole clothes.

Hipster comeback

This outfit of 2002 is by Spanish-born designer Amaya Arzuaga (b.1971). The low-slung skirt and halter-neck top reveal plenty of bare flesh.

Ethnic styles

THROUGHOUT THE HISTORY OF EUROPEAN DRESS, *clothes have drawn from other cultures. The East has always been a source of exotic fabrics. The Silk Road, originally used by ancient Roman traders to carry silks from China, was reopened in the 1400s.*

East meets West

Later, there was a trend for traditional Indian textiles, thanks to trade fostered by the East India Company (1600–1708). At the Great Exhibition (1851), fabrics from all corners of the British Empire were displayed. A key importer of oriental fabrics was Arthur Lasenby Liberty (1843–1917). His Liberty store opened in London in 1875, selling Persian cashmere, crepe from Japan and silk from China and India.

KIMONOS FROM JAPAN

A pure silk kimono, as shown in this 19th-century illustration, is still the traditional choice for Japanese women attending special ceremonies. It is worn with a broad, four-metre-long sash called an obi, tied in an elaborate bow. In the West, the kimono inspired the boudoir gowns of the early 1900s, and dressing-gowns of the 1920s.

JAPANESE DESIGN TODAY

Since the 1970s, Japanese designers have found worldwide success. Like many of his contemporaries, Kansai Yamamoto (b.1944) learned how to structure his clothes by looking at traditional Japanese dress. Mixing in modern details, Yamamoto creates elegant dresses in a clean, uncluttered style (right).

LAURA ASHLEY & THE GYPSY LOOK

This pretty dress from the 1970s is by Laura Ashley (1925–85). Ashley started out by selling gypsy-style printed headscarves and many of her clothing collections were inspired by peasant dress.

Ethnic in the 1960s...

In its widest sense, ethnic style means dress that belongs to a particular culture. Always on the lookout for new inspiration, designers have scoured every corner of the world, stealing dress styles, fabrics, or even just motifs. Ethnic styling really hit the mainstream in the 1960s. Soon all the trendiest stalls and boutiques were selling imported clothes – embroidered kaftans and cheesecloth skirts.

... & 1970s

Soon the ethnic look filtered up to haute couture design! Louis Feraud (*b.*1921) designed a collection based on American Indian clothes, while Yves Saint Laurent drew on Russian peasant dress.

Ethnic nostalgia

In the early 21st century, designers returned to the peasant styles last popular in the 1970s. This gypsy outfit was shown on the Paris catwalks for Spring/Summer 2002.

Children's dresses

CHILDREN'S CLOTHES REFLECT THE SOCIETIES THEY LIVE IN. *Until the end of the 18th century, babies and young children were dressed in long gowns worn over swaddling clothes. Swaddling clothes were like bandages, which wrapped up the baby, protecting its arms and legs. Once free of these clothes, girls faired little better. They were put into restrictive dresses that were miniature copies of their mothers'.*

BOYS WILL BE GIRLS

In the 1600s boys wore dresses until they were breeched – put in a pair of breeches (trousers). Over the following centuries, breeching took place earlier and earlier until gowns were reserved for baby girls.

Modest movement

At the beginning of the 19th century fashions were changing. Girls began to wear less awkward dresses, but modesty was still very important. Pantalets (drawers) were introduced to be worn under dresses. Trimmed with pretty pin tucks or lace, pantalets reached the ankles. They meant a girl could raise her skirts for easier movement – without offending anyone with a show of leg!

TRADITIONAL CHRISTENING ROBE, 1863

Traditionally, long white robes were worn by baby boys and girls for their christening. Made in fine laces and embroidery, such robes often became family heirlooms, handed down through the generations.

24

Frills & flounces

The Victorians adored frills and flounces! Compared to the mass-produced clothes of today, Victorian childrenswear was expensive. For this reason, clothes had deep tucks, big hems and wide seams so that they could be adapted to fit as the child grew.

When playing, girls often wore pinafores to protect their dresses or smocks. The smock was based on the garments worn by farm-workers over their clothes. It was gathered at the top, or yoke, and had puffed sleeves. Usually home-sewn, it often had decorative embroidery over the smocking gathers.

Victorian girl in pantalets

Girls' dresses were full like their mothers' but shorter for easier movement. Pretty pantalets were worn underneath to keep the legs modestly covered.

French childrenswear

In the 1930s, girls' dresses followed the same curvy lines as adult womenswear.

Child-friendly

In the 20th century, companies began to specialize in childrenswear, but styles remained easier-to-wear versions of adult fashions. Prices came down thanks to mass-production. From the 1950s, the sportier adult styles crossed over into children's dress, resulting in more comfort than ever before. Around this period, designers saw the potential of the teen market. Boutiques opened that sold clothes designed just for teenagers.

Sweet smock

A children's book illustration of a typical toddler's smock of the mid-20th century.

Men in skirts

WE USUALLY THINK OF THE SKIRT AS A GARMENT FOR WOMEN *but men have long worn skirts – from simple grass skirts to pleated kilts. Skirts for men are part of the traditional national dress in a number of countries. The white, pleated fustanella is still part of the uniform of the Greek national guard, worn for special occasions.*

Cool linen

High-ranking ancient Egyptian men wore wrapped skirts that were sometimes pleated. Made of fine linen, these wrapped skirts would have been comfortably cool in the Egyptian heat.

The fustanella

This white, pleated kilt remains the national dress for Greek and Albanian men. Its name comes from fustian, the coarse cotton cloth used to make it.

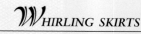

Whirling skirts

The Islamic whirling dervishes (founded in 1273) are famed for their wild dancing. Spinning in swirling skirts, they enter a trance, hoping to come closer to Allah.

The kilt

One of the best-known men's skirts is the tartan kilt. Tartan is a checked, woollen cloth from Scotland. It is believed the cloth may date back to the 1400s and today there are more than 1,300 recorded styles. Each highland clan, or family, has its own tartan with its own colouring and style of check. The kilt is now part of Scotland's national dress, worn worldwide by people of Scottish ancestry. Since the 1980s the kilt has re-emerged as a sign of Scottish national pride. It is especially popular among young football supporters. Wearing kilts to matches, they have been nicknamed the 'tartan army'.

HIGHLAND DRESS, C.1902

It takes nearly seven metres of cloth to make the traditional kilt, which is flat-fronted with pleats at the back. The kilt is worn with a matching length of plaid that pins at the shoulder. A fur pouch called a sporran hangs from the belt at the front.

JEAN-PAUL GAULTIER KILT

Gaultier's designs often shock! This pleated mini is his fun update of the kilt.

Men's skirts in haute couture

Today, skirts for men are high fashion. Jean-Paul Gaultier (*b.*1952), known for his witty, sexy designs, has included kilts in his menswear collections. Short and showy, his creations are too outrageous for most men. Simple wraparounds based on the sarong have proved easier to wear. One of the most famous men to wear one is footballer David Beckham (*b.*1975).

Fashionable technology

UNTIL THE 1800S ALL GARMENTS WERE HAND-SEWN, *whether they were the work of master tailors or home seamstresses. The coming of the sewing-machine revolutionized the business of making clothes. Clothes could be put together more quickly, cheaply and easily than ever before.*

Birth of the sewing-machine

From the late 1700s, various inventors tried to design a machine that could mimic hand-stitching. This was finally achieved by the American Elias Howe (1819–67), who patented his sewing-machine in 1846. Millions of machines sold worldwide. Factories equipped with sewing-machines could turn out garments at high speed. As production rose, prices fell and fashion became more affordable for the masses.

MASTER TAILOR OF THE 1640S

Cutting clothes that will hang well requires great skill. In the past, tailors served as unpaid apprentices while learning their craft.

THE FIRST SEWING-MACHINE

Elias Howe unveiled his machine in 1845. It made 200 stitches a minute – seven times as fast as any seamstress! Along with the invention of the paper dress pattern, the sewing-machine made home dressmaking far easier.

SWEAT SHOP LABOUR

The 1800s saw the birth of the sweat shop, where many women worked in terrible factories. Sweat shops still exist, with machinists working long hours for little pay.

Fabulous new fabrics

The creation of new, man-made materials also had a huge impact on dressmaking. The first was rayon. Cheap to produce, it looked like silk or satin and was first used commercially in the early 1900s.

Synthetic materials, such as nylon and polyester, have other advantages besides cost. They may not crease like cotton or silk, nor lose their shape like wool. Mixing them with natural fibres produces materials that keep the best aspects of both. Synthetic Lycra gives superb stretchiness – ideal when making dresses that fit well, but are also comfortable to wear.

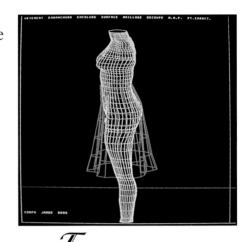

THE COMPUTER AGE

Computers are a great design tool. They can show how a finished dress will look, and even create an exact pattern for the cutters to follow.

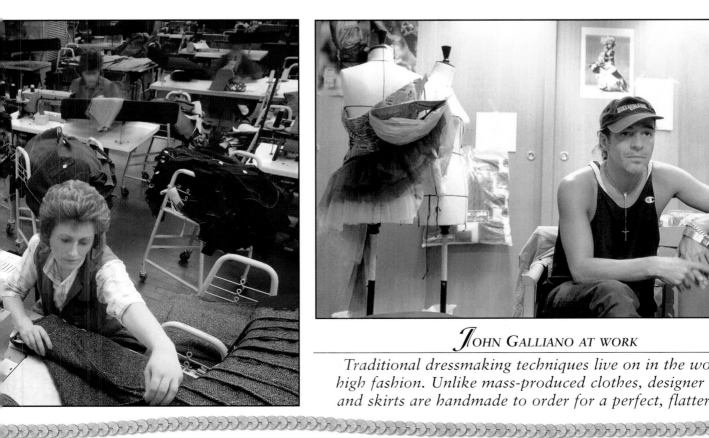

PLATED METAL BY PACO RABANNE

Spanish-born Rabanne (b.1934) is famous for making dresses in highly unusual materials, such as metal, paper and plastics.

JOHN GALLIANO AT WORK

Traditional dressmaking techniques live on in the world of high fashion. Unlike mass-produced clothes, designer dresses and skirts are handmade to order for a perfect, flattering fit.

Timeline

Prehistory
The first garments were made of skin and later, woven cloth wrapped around the body.

The ancient world
The ancient Egyptians, Greeks and Romans all had highly stylized versions of the tunic and wrap.

The Middle Ages
Tunics were simplified and long sleeves were added. By the 1400s, the dress was shaped to fit the body. Waist girdles accentuated the natural waist. The fashionable neckline lowered and sleeves were long and flowing.

16th century
The fashionable dress had a structured shape and was made in heavy silks and velvets. Bodices were stiff and long, ending in a 'V' at the front. The bell-shaped skirt was left open in front to reveal the petticoat. In the second half of the century, ruffs became popular. Made of starched materials they could encircle the neck or be left open. Dresses had enormous, leg-of-mutton sleeves and skirts were held out by the farthingale (a hooped underskirt made of whalebone).

17th century
Lighter fabrics were in fashion so farthingales were no longer necessary. Waistlines rose. The ruff was replaced with collars of linen and lace. Sleeves ended at the elbow with lace cuffs.

18th century
The fashionable woman began to wear a hoop under her skirts, which were again made of rich, heavy fabrics. The hoop was later replaced with a pannier each side of the hips, making dresses wide and narrow. Then, while heavy brocades remained popular at court, fashionable society wore dresses made from light, hand-painted silks, muslins and lawns. While the necklines of evening-dresses were revealing, day dresses were often worn with a kerchief to cover the bare neck. The loose-fitting sack gown, which had box pleats falling down the back, was worn at home. At the end of the century, hoops disappeared as dresses took inspiration from classical times.

19th century
At the beginning of the century, high-waisted classical dress remained fashionable. Long, slim evening-dresses had low, square necklines and short, puffed sleeves. As the century progressed, the line of the waist dropped and so did the sleeve seam, resulting in sloping shoulders. By 1850, the numerous heavy petticoats were replaced by the crinoline cage – resulting in skirts of enormous widths. Within a decade the fullness moved to the back with the introduction of the crinolette and, later, the bustle. Towards the end of the century, fashionable women wore the S-line dress. Blouses, fitted jackets and long skirts were popular.

20th century & beyond
Campaigns by dress reformers led to more comfortable fashions. By the 1920s, hems had risen to the knee. The waistline also dropped, creating a tubular shape that hid the bust and hips. The 1930s saw the return of feminine curves, and the backless evening-dress was popular. In 1947 the New Look was introduced with its small, wasp waists and billowing skirts. In the 1960s the mini-dress came in. Long, peasant skirts were popular in the 1970s. The next decade saw the successful woman in a power suit, which had a short, slim skirt. Eveningwear was romantic, with full, puffed-out skirts. In the 1990s, and at the start of the 21st century, the emphasis was on individual style. Anything went – skirts could be full or slim, sweeping the floor or barely covering the knickers!

Glossary

Box pleat

Two folds made in the fabric to meet each other in the middle of the pleat.

Bustle

Padding worn under the skirt to push it out at the back. Bustle skirts were in fashion during the 1860s and 1870s.

Crepe

Fabric, especially silk, that has been heat-treated to create a crinkled texture.

Crimplene

An easy-care, man-made fabric popular during the 1960s.

Crinoline

A frame of hoops made of whalebone or steel. Crinolines were used from the 1850s to hold out enormously wide skirts.

Cut on the bias

A garment made from fabric that has been cut in a diagonal line, or across the grain, so that it falls in soft folds.

Gabardine

A dense fabric that has a fine diagonal rib effect, popular for suits, coats and skirts.

Girdle

A cord that encircled the waist. It was used as a belt for the medieval tunic dress.

Gore

A dressmaking method to create fullness without the use of pleats or gathers. Gored skirts have a sewn-in panel, producing a close fit at the waist and a flared hem.

Haute couture

French for 'high dressmaking'; one-off garments that are constructed to the client's personal measurements. The workmanship of haute couture is usually superb.

Lawn

Very fine, crisp cotton or linen, often bleached white then printed.

Pin tuck

A narrow (pin-sized) fold of fabric, held in place with a row of stitches. Rows of pin tucks often decorate blouses or petticoats.

Smocking

Decorative stitches to hold in fullness. First used on labourers' smocks, it decorated the yoke of children's dresses from the 19th century onwards.

Twinset

A matching jumper and cardigan, first invented by the Scottish knitwear firm Pringle in the 1920s.

Index

A-line 10
animal skins 4–5, 30
Ashley, Laura 22

bias-cut 11, 31
bloomer outfit 14
bodice 12, 16, 20, 30
bustle 10, 12, 30–31

Chanel, Coco 11, 15, 16–17
childrenswear 24–25
christening gown 24
computer 7, 29
Courrèges, André 11
crepe 22, 31
Crimplene 9, 31
crinoline 12–13, 18, 30–31

Delphos dress 19
Dior, Christian 10, 13
directoire dress 12

Egyptians 6, 18, 26, 30
evening-dress 5, 20–21, 30

farthingale 30
Feraud, Louis 23
flapper 13, 29
Fortuny, Mariano 19
fustanella 26

gabardine 9, 31
Gaultier, Jean-Paul 27
Gibson Girl 20
girdle 8, 30–31
gore 10, 31
Greeks 4, 6, 8, 30
Grès, Alix 7
gym skirt 18
gypsy style 22–23

hobble skirt 16

kilt 26–27
kimono 22

Lagerfeld, Karl 15
lawn 14, 18, 31
Liberty, Arthur Lasenby 22
Lycra 5, 17, 29

man-made fabric 5, 9, 29
menswear 26–27
mini 9, 11, 21, 30
Minoans 20

New Look 13, 30

pantalets 24–25
Patou, Jean 16
pencil skirt 17
pin tuck 24, 31
pleat 9, 16, 18–19, 26–27, 30–31
Poiret, Paul 9, 16

power dressing 15, 30
princess dress 10

Quant, Mary 21

Rabanne, Paco 29
Rational Dress Society 14
Romans 6, 8, 12, 22, 30

sack dress 18, 30
Saint Laurent, Yves 15, 23
sari 7
sarong 7, 27
Schiaparelli, Elsa 11
sewing-machine 28
smocking 25, 31
suit 14–15, 31
sweat shop 28

tailor 5, 7, 10, 12, 28
tartan 26
toga 6
tunic 4, 8–9, 10, 30–31
twinset 17, 31

Utility clothing 14

Vionnet, Madeleine 11

Westwood, Vivienne 15
Worth, Charles Frederick 12, 20

Yamamoto, Kansai 22